D1717140

DOLLARS AND SENSE
A GUIDE TO FINANCIAL LITERACY ™

Savings and Investments

DAVID W. BERG AND
MEG GREEN

NEW YORK

Published in 2012 by The Rosen Publishing Group, Inc.
29 East 21st Street, New York, NY 10010

Library of Congress Cataloging-in-Publication Data

Berg, David W.
Savings and investments/David W. Berg, Meg Green.—1st ed.
    p. cm.—(Dollars and sense: a guide to financial literacy)
Includes bibliographical references and index.
ISBN 978-1-4488-4712-9 (library binding)
ISBN 978-1-4488-4722-8 (pbk.)
ISBN 978-1-4488-4754-9 (6-pack)
1. Saving and investment—Juvenile literature. 2. Investments—Juvenile literature. 3. Finance, Personal—Juvenile literature. I. Green, Meg. II. Title.
HG4521.B437 2012
332.024—dc22

                                                                2010051938

Manufactured in the United States of America

CPSIA Compliance Information: Batch #S11YA: For further information, contact Rosen Publishing, New York, New York, at 1-800-237-9932.

CONTENTS

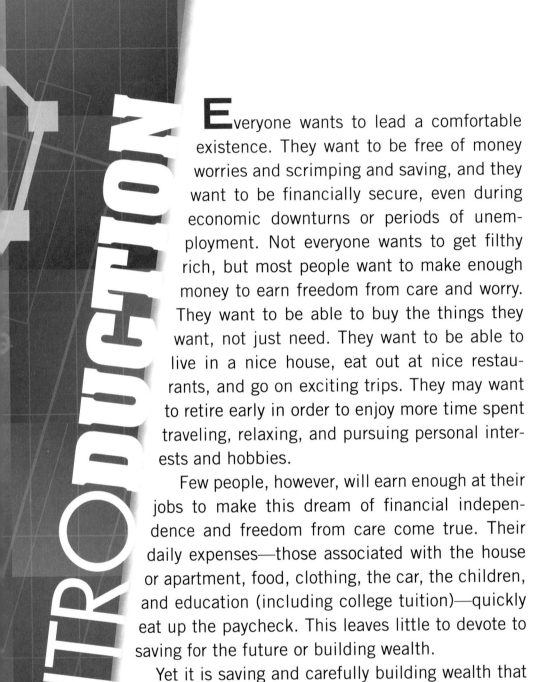

Everyone wants to lead a comfortable existence. They want to be free of money worries and scrimping and saving, and they want to be financially secure, even during economic downturns or periods of unemployment. Not everyone wants to get filthy rich, but most people want to make enough money to earn freedom from care and worry. They want to be able to buy the things they want, not just need. They want to be able to live in a nice house, eat out at nice restaurants, and go on exciting trips. They may want to retire early in order to enjoy more time spent traveling, relaxing, and pursuing personal interests and hobbies.

Few people, however, will earn enough at their jobs to make this dream of financial independence and freedom from care come true. Their daily expenses—those associated with the house or apartment, food, clothing, the car, the children, and education (including college tuition)—quickly eat up the paycheck. This leaves little to devote to saving for the future or building wealth.

Yet it is saving and carefully building wealth that will make the dream of financial security and independence a reality. Most of the world's millionaires and billionaires achieved their wealth by saving and investing their money, one dime at a dime, one dollar

Spending money is easy, but saving it can be a challenge. It requires discipline, patience, and long-range planning.

at a time. Yet in a recent survey, 27 percent of adults said their best chance of acquiring half a million dollars or more in their lifetime was by winning the lottery. The sad and sobering reality is that a person is more likely to get hit by lightning than win the lottery. The other side of that coin, however, is that the best bet for anyone seeking to build wealth and establish financial security is to save and invest his or her money.

There is no complicated formula or insider secret to becoming wealthy and secure. Selena Maranjian, a financial adviser who writes for the Motley Fool, an online site that teaches people how to invest, says, "Kids are almost guaranteed to become millionaires if they regularly save and invest a small amount of money…The more you can learn about it, the better, and the earlier you start, the better. If you start saving and investing when you are fifteen, by the time you're sixty-five you'll have an amazing amount of money."

The time to start saving and investing is today. Read on to learn how to go about doing it safely and wisely and how to create the secure, comfortable, and enriching life that you want for yourself and your loved ones.

CHAPTER ONE

MONEY MANAGEMENT 101: BUILDING WEALTH

It can take years of saving and investing to become wealthy and financially independent, but the earlier you start, the sooner you'll reach your goal. The one thing that millionaires have in common is they watch how they spend their money. They decide what is more important: something they want today or something they may need tomorrow. To do this, they create and stick to budgets, which are detailed plans for how they will spend, save, and invest the money that is available to them.

The first step to building wealth is simply to start saving money. Every penny counts. Most kids receive some money through gifts, allowances, or jobs. No matter how you get your money, you can start to make a plan for using it, as opposed to simply spending it. Your money can be used to make more money. If you spend it, however, it's gone and never coming back.

Keep Your Eye on the Prize

Don't think of budgeting as going on a financial diet. Instead, think of it as setting aside a couple of pieces of pie for later when you are really hungry and will really be able to savor and appreciate them. Motivate yourself by keeping in mind your ultimate goal, whether it's setting aside enough cash for a new mountain bike, planning a postgraduation trip to Europe, saving for college, or planning for an early retirement (financial advisers will tell you that it's never too early to begin planning for retirement). And remember, the money you set aside today could grow, making for an even larger pie tomorrow.

All wealth begins not with spending but with saving. There's no mysterious secret to learn, no intricate trick to master, no get-rich-quick scheme to invest in. It just requires discipline, hard work, and a long-term outlook. "The key thing to remember is saving is a habit," says Irene Leech, a professor of consumer studies at Virginia Tech and a consumer education specialist with the Virginia Cooperative Extension. "It's something everyone, kids and adults, needs to work on."

For example, if you save just $5 a week, you would have set aside $260 in a year, $1,300 in five years, and $2,600

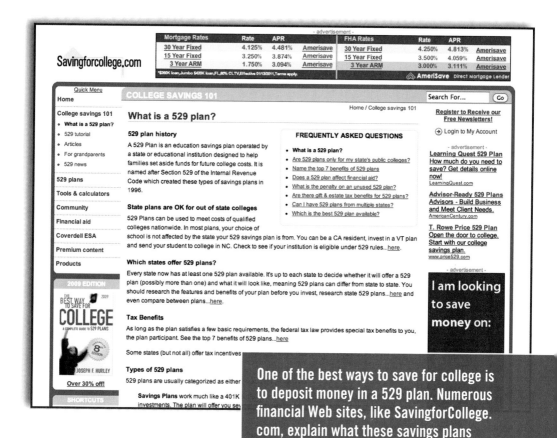

One of the best ways to save for college is to deposit money in a 529 plan. Numerous financial Web sites, like SavingforCollege.com, explain what these savings plans are, how they work, and how to set one up.

in ten years. However, if you deposit your $5 a week in a savings account that earns 6 percent interest that's compounded, or added, annually, you would earn $275.60 in a year, $1,547.22 in five years, and $3,624.06 in ten years.

If it's smart to save money, it's also smart to spend your money wisely. It's a good idea to engage in a "cooling off" period when considering a purchase. Don't buy anything over $30 to $50 without taking at least twenty-four hours to think about it. This will help you avoid impulse purchases that are neither truly wanted nor needed.

CARVING UP THE PIE

Think of your money as a pie, and cut your pieces carefully and thoughtfully. Some financial advisers recommend saving about one-third of your discretionary income (money not devoted to day-to-day essentials like food and bills) for long-term goals, like college tuition, a first home, or even retirement. Another third of the money should be saved for short-term goals, like buying a new bike, video game, or music download. For the remaining third, some people like to set aside a percentage for charitable organizations and the rest for small expenses, like movie tickets or a restaurant dinner.

If that plan is too strict for you, consider putting aside just 10 percent of your discretionary income for saving and investing. You can always increase this percentage as you get more comfortable with and knowledgeable about saving and investing. But it's important to start getting in the saving habit immediately, even if you're only setting aside a small percentage of your available cash.

To the Cheap Go the Spoils

Instead of spending $70 on a new pair of blue jeans at a department store, you could buy a barely used pair from a thrift store for $10 or find steeply discounted brand-name jeans online. Instead of spending $10 to eat lunch out, bring a sandwich from home. Instead of spending $12 to go to a first-run movie, you could spend $2 or $3 renting it, legally downloading it, or watching it on demand through pay television. In many cases, first-run movies are released simultaneously to theaters, video, and pay television, so you wouldn't even have to wait a few weeks to view it less expensively outside the theater.

In addition, many goods and services, including things like concert or sports tickets, can be purchased online through auction or classified advertisement sites, like eBay and Craigslist. Sometimes prices for items sold on these sites will be higher than retail if the demand is high and the supply is low. Other times, however, people are looking to quickly unload goods they can't use or don't want, and great bargains can be found.

When you decide there is something you really do want to buy, shop around to find the best price. This includes both

It is wise to limit purchases to those things you truly need, and to shop around for the best discounts and sales.

brick-and-mortar stores (such as department stores, special-ized shops and boutiques, superstores or big-box stores [like Walmart, Sam's Club, and Target]), and discounters and wholesalers. Something at one store or online retailer may be cheaper at a different store or Web site. In addition, competi-tors may promise to match the lowest price you have found elsewhere, so don't be afraid to haggle.

Tracking Expenses

To increase your mindfulness and deliberateness about spend-ing and avoid frittering your money away, it's a good idea to write down what you've done with your cash each time you spend it. You can use a notebook to write down what money you receive (through gifts, allowance, work around the house, or paychecks, for example) and where you put it—whether you invest it in stocks, keep it in your bank account, or spend it on video games and fast food. You may keep a separate journal to keep track of individual investments. You should also save all of your receipts in envelopes, one for every month.

Keeping records of how you spend your money is very important. It is an essential skill you will use the rest of your life. Sloppy bookkeeping can cost you money. If you lose a bill and don't pay it on time, you may face heavy financial penal-ties. You can't touch some investments until a certain period of time has passed or you will get hit with steep early with-drawal charges. This is why it's important to know exactly how much money you have, where it is, what the various rules are

Having a credit card doesn't mean you can buy something you couldn't otherwise afford. It should be used only as a convenience—when carrying cash is impractical, for example—or in emergencies.

for these banking and investment accounts, how much money you need, and where you will draw it from without incurring any financial penalties.

Writing down where your money goes is also a good way for you to chart exactly how you are spending it. Did you know that spending $1.50 to buy a can of soda every day means you're spending $547.50 a year on sugar, syrup, and carbonated water? Maybe you'd rather spend that money on a new snowboard or put it toward paying for college.

Now that you are ready to save money, let's talk about how you can invest it and let it grow for you!

CHAPTER TWO

MAKING YOUR MONEY GROW: EARNED INTEREST AND ROI

"**M**oney is a terrible master, but an excellent servant," said P. T. Barnum, the legendary circus owner and promoter. What he meant was that if you do not manage money wisely and end up without enough to meet your needs, you become a slave to economic forces and labor mightily to stay afloat. If you manage money wisely, however, the things it does for you—and allows you to do—can be wonderfully fulfilling and of great value to yourself, your family, and society at large.

Saving money is a great habit to get into because it builds a nice cushion of security. It creates reserves of cash against a "rainy day"—an economic downturn, a sudden and unexpected large expense, or prolonged unemployment. Yet most savings accounts offer a relatively low return on investment (ROI). Interest rates for savings accounts tend to be only about 1 to 2 percent compounded annually. This means that if you deposit $100 in a savings account on January 1, by the next New Year's Day you will have earned only one or two dollars in interest. If you invest some—not all!—of your savings, however, you may earn a far higher rate of return. Your money can be put to work to make more money—sometimes a lot more money. This is one way to turn money into your servant.

The Risks and Rewards of Investing

Investing is using money like a magnet to attract more money. Have you ever heard that money doesn't grow on trees? It doesn't, but it can be used as a seed to grow more money. The income that your seed money earns is called interest, or return. Some investments, like a savings account, promise to give your seed money back, plus interest, at the end of a period of time. Other investments, like some stocks, offer no guarantees that you'll get your seed money back at all. You may earn nothing or even lose money. You must be crazy to risk losing your seed money, right?

That's where investing gets tricky. It may sound crazy to put your seed money at risk. Yet by doing so, you could earn a higher return and your money could grow faster. You have to

Day-to-day stock prices can be very volatile. In the long run, however, stocks generally offer the best return on investment.

research the risks of each investment you are considering and decide what kind of risk you are willing to take. The good news is that some investments get less risky the longer you hang on to them. And as a teen, that's one thing you've got going for you: the luxury of time.

Interest Rates and Returns

When you invest money—whether in a savings account or stocks and bonds—you can earn interest. To calculate interest, you multiply the dollar amount by the percentage of interest. For instance, to find the interest earned on a onetime investment of $100 invested at an annual rate of 5 percent, you would multiply $100 by 5 percent, or .05. That would be $5 in interest earned your first year. So after a year, your $100 seed money would have grown to $105.

Just as a magnet grows more powerful as it gets bigger, the bigger your cash reserve gets, the harder it can work for you and the faster it can grow by attracting more money. That's the magic of compound interest, which is the return that your interest earns.

TIME IS ON YOUR MONEY'S SIDE

Benjamin Franklin once said, "Time is money." He was right; the longer you keep your investments, the more your money grows. Here's an example:

- Save $25 a week and invest it at 5 percent, and it will grow to $166,020 over forty years.
- Save $25 a week and invest it at 7 percent, and it will grow to $286,030 over forty years.
- Save $50 a week and invest it at 5 percent, and it will grow to $332,020 over forty years.
- Save $50 a week and invest it at 9 percent, and it will grow to $1,021,910 over forty years. If you had just tucked that $50 a week into a shoe box, you'd have only $104,000 in forty years, about one-tenth of what you earned with a 9 percent interest rate.

To compound the interest, you calculate future interest based on your principal and what return your principal has earned so far. So, using the above example, in the second year of your investment you start off with $105. Multiply $105 by the 5 percent interest rate. The result shows that in your second year, you will earn $5.25 in interest. Add that to your $105, and now you have $110.25 at the end of your second year. In the third year, you'd multiply $110.25 by 5 percent to earn $5.51 in interest. Now you have $115.76. See how it works? In three years, you've earned $15.76 without lifting a finger. The more money you have earning interest, the greater your returns. If you had deposited $1,000 in an account earning 5 percent interest annually, you would have earned $157.63 in three years and now have an account worth $1,157.63. If you kept that original $100 invested at 5 percent, it would grow to $322.40 in twenty-five years. A thousand dollars would grow to $3,224.

Fighting Inflation by Saving Early

Earning interest can help you fight inflation. "Inflation" is a term that describes how things get more expensive every year. A few years ago, you could get a can of soda from a vending machine for about 45 cents. Now the price is $1.25, $1.50, or even higher. This means your money doesn't go as far as it used to. Prices rise, and the purchasing power of a dollar bill decreases. A dollar will not be able to buy as much as it used to when prices rise. So the trick is to have your investments

Be sure to keep careful track of all deposits, withdrawals, check and debit payments, bank fees, and interest earned in order to properly balance your checking account and accurately monitor your finances.

increase in value along with rising prices. This way the investments keep up with or even surpass the rate of inflation. Three factors determine how investments grow: how big the principal is, how much time it has to grow, and what interest rate it grows at.

Because time is a major factor in how investments grow, the earlier you start saving and investing, the better. If you waited until you were thirty-five to invest $100 at a 20 percent rate of return, it could grow to $9,540 by the time you turned sixty. But if you invested $100 when you were fifteen at that same rate of return, by the time you were sixty you'd have $365,726.

Even if your investment had a lower rate of return, say 10 percent, if you invested that $100 at age twenty-five you'd have $1,083 when you were sixty. But if you invested $100 at 10 percent when you were fifteen, you'd have $7,289 by the time you turned sixty.

CHAPTER THREE

LOW-RISK SAVING AND INVESTMENT OPPORTUNITIES

Short-term, low-risk investments are the best option when you want to both protect and grow your money with virtually no chance of losses. These are a good choice if you're trying to raise money for desired purchases, like a new computer, for example.

Most financial advisers will tell you that the place to go for safe, short-term investment of savings is a bank. There are several different places, or accounts, where you can deposit your money in the bank; most will require permission from a parent or guardian.

22

Depositing Money in a Savings Account

A savings account is like your own personal piggy bank, except you keep your cash at the bank, where it is safe from thieves—including brothers and sisters—and earns some interest. After filling out some paperwork at the bank, you'll get either a passbook savings account or a regular savings account. Both come with little ledger books to keep track of what money you put into the bank, what you take out, and what interest you earn.

With a passbook savings account, you bring the book to the bank every time you make a deposit, or put money into

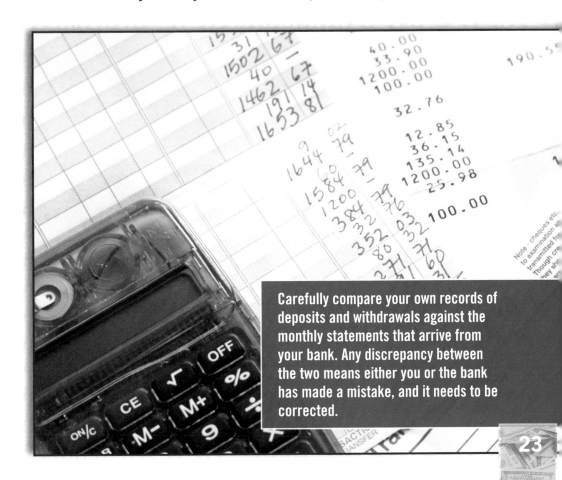

Carefully compare your own records of deposits and withdrawals against the monthly statements that arrive from your bank. Any discrepancy between the two means either you or the bank has made a mistake, and it needs to be corrected.

the account, and every time you withdraw, or take money from the account. The bank teller creates an itemized record of all your banking activity—the deposits and withdrawals—in the passbook.

With a regular savings account, it's up to you to keep track of your deposits and withdrawals. You'll have to fill out a little slip of paper every time you make a deposit or withdrawal in person, and update your ledger book yourself. If you use an automated teller machine (ATM), you will receive a receipt for your transaction, and you must then record that transaction in your ledger book. The bank will also keep a record of all your transactions. With either a passbook or regular savings account, you'll get a printout, or statement, from the bank every month or every quarter (every three months). The statement will show your balance, or how much is in your account, plus any deposits, withdrawals, or interest earned in that time period.

Savings accounts are pretty simple, and you can withdraw money anytime you like. You may need to keep a minimum amount of money in your account, however, to avoid extra service charges and penalties. Shop around and talk to a few banks to find the highest interest rate you can.

Earning More Interest: Money Market Funds

A money market fund is similar to a savings account, except the bank invests the money in short-term investments, like bonds, to make a profit. A money market fund is actually a form of mutual fund. In a money market, your money may earn a higher interest rate than in a standard savings account, but a money market account may have more restrictions. Some banks require a minimum deposit before you can open a money market account, and some limit how many times a month or year you can withdraw money from the account.

HOW THE GOVERNMENT RAISES MONEY: U.S. SAVINGS BONDS

The federal government raises money by selling U.S. savings bonds, which you can also buy at the bank or even online. By buying a bond, you are loaning your money to the United States government for a certain period of time. In return, when you cash the bond, you earn interest on your investment.

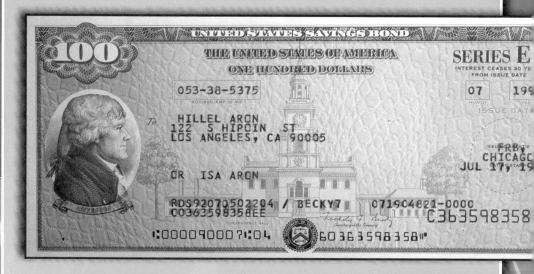

Savings bonds offer generally safe and reliable investment opportunities and returns on investment while also helping fund important and useful public and government projects.

25

Time to Grow: Certificates of Deposit

A certificate of deposit, or CD, is similar to a money market fund. Banks also usually require you to deposit a minimum amount in a certificate of deposit. But a CD may have even more restrictions on when you can take your money out.

In return for a favorable interest rate, you agree to keep your money in the CD for a certain length of time—from three months to three years. It's a safe place to set aside money that you know you won't need for a while.

A Solid Foundation

Investing is like a ladder. You want to establish a solid, low-risk basis for your money before you reach for higher, riskier investments. The above investments are a good place for a new investor to start, and you will always want to keep some of your money in these safe places. But once you have established your investing and saving foundation, you may want to consider using some of your money to take on investments with greater risk—and greater rewards.

CHAPTER FOUR

HIGHER-RISK INVESTMENT OPTIONS

To make an investment and to earn interest or a return on it, you have to allow others to use your seed money, or principal, to build their business. You are in a sense loaning them money to fund their business operations, and you hope to receive that loan back with interest. You are also essentially betting on the future success of the company, product, project, or enterprise in which you are investing. All investments come with a certain amount of risk, so it's important to understand what that risk is.

There are seven basic types of investments: banks, stocks, bonds, mutual funds, real estate, commodities, and collectibles. Some are riskier than others, and some are easier than others for young people to invest in. For some investments, anyone under the age of eighteen may need the help or permission of a parent or other responsible adult.

Money in the Bank

Banks, credit unions, and savings and loans provide the most basic way of saving and investing money. They are all private institutions where people can keep and grow their money. These financial institutions differ in who runs them and who regulates them, but mostly they offer the same types of saving and investing possibilities.

Banks are in business to make money and are owned by private companies. Credit unions are owned by their members, who pool their money together to offer loans to each other. Savings and loans can be owned by either a private company or an association of members.

Your money is safe in a bank because it's protected by insurance. Most banks are protected by the Federal Deposit Insurance Corporation, while credit unions are protected by the National Credit Union Share Insurance Fund. If the bank or credit union goes bankrupt, the U.S. government will make sure you get your money back, up to $250,000. Non-interest-bearing accounts (like checking accounts) are fully insured, meaning the account holder would receive all of his or her

Most banks prominently display their status as FDIC insured. When shopping around for a bank in which to place your money, be sure to ask if your deposits are insured by the federal government.

money back, no matter how large the account. Some savings and loans are not required to have deposit insurance, but most have it anyway. This is a good business decision because most people would not feel safe putting their money in an unin- sured bank, and they'd take their money to a properly insured financial institution instead. If you or your parents choose a savings and loan, ask the bank representative if deposits are protected by insurance.

While banks have your deposited money, they use it to make loans to other people. They pay you interest for letting them keep your money for a while, then they make loans to other people at a higher interest rate. So they get paid back more money than they lend over time. This is one way they make a profit. In return for the money you've loaned them, they give you a piece of the action in the form of interest, though this is a pretty small piece. That means the interest rate they pay you is usually fairly low. Often the interest rate is lower than the inflation rate, meaning the money you earn in interest will not help you keep up with rising prices.

Buying and Selling Stocks

Buying stock means becoming part-owner of a company. Stockholders, also called shareholders, share in the compa- ny's success or failure. If the company makes money, you will share in its profit. If the company loses money, you will share in its losses. As a shareholder, you can vote on certain things that the company proposes to do. The number of votes you

Any company that issues ownership shares—or stocks—that are traded in an open market like a stock exchange is considered a publicly traded company. These stock certificates are proof of an investor's part-ownership in the companies and represent his or her financial stake in their success or failure.

have is based on the number of shares of stock you have. Stocks change in price as they are bought and sold on the stock market, which is a type of auction.

Historically, out of all the various kinds of investment opportunities and venues, the stock market has the best rate

31

of return in the long run. In the short term, however, stock prices rise and fall every day. If you're looking for a quick profit, you could just as likely experience a quick loss of your investment value. Over time—years and decades—stock prices for any given reputable, well-managed, innovative company tend to rise. Over the short term, however—days and months—that same company may experience sharp fluctuations in share price. So stocks should generally be considered a long-term investment.

Buy Bonds

Bonds are another way companies and governments raise money. Bonds are a type of loan, except instead of going to the bank to get it, companies and governments go to private investors. Treasury bills, called T-bills, are short-term loans to the government (for periods of less than a year). Treasury bonds, called T-bonds, are long-term loans to the federal government (ten years or more). If the government needs to raise $10 million to fund infrastructure projects (bridges, tunnels, highways, etc.), it can divide that $10 million into 1,000 bonds worth $10,000 each or 10,000 bonds worth $1,000 each. People who buy the bonds are guaranteed a certain return at the end of a set time period, say ten years. Over that ten-year period, the bondholders receive interest payments, just like they do from a bank.

The downside of bonds is that if you sell yours before the ten-year period is up, you may face financial penalties. Also, some bonds are riskier than others, which is something to be aware of. Except for U.S. Savings Bonds, most bonds require a high deposit and aren't very easy for teens to invest in directly.

Diving in the Mutual Fund Pool

Mutual funds are formed by a team of individual investors who pool their money together to buy a collection of stocks or bonds. A mutual fund company has a professional manager who picks which companies to invest in or which bonds to buy. As an investor, you buy a piece of the mutual fund, and you share in the profits or losses of the fund as a whole. It's an easy way to invest because someone else—the fund manager—worries full-time about which investment opportunities might be profitable and which may lose money. You can just sit back, let someone else do the research and make the decisions, and hopefully watch your money grow.

EXPENSIVE TOYS: COLLECTIBLES

Collectibles, like comics, *Star Wars* toys, and baseball cards, may seem like a fun way to invest. Something you bought for $3 today might be worth $300 tomorrow. And you may feel safer being able to actually see, touch, and possess your investment, unlike the money you put into a bank, stocks, or a mutual fund.

But collectibles may not be the best way to invest your money. It's difficult to know what kind of collectibles will be valuable ten, twenty, or thirty years from now. Plus, for many collectibles to be valuable in the future, they must be in mint, or unused, condition. And what fun is a toy if you can't play with it?

The flip side of this is that, in a mutual fund, you don't have as much control over your individual investment and might not even know what companies the mutual fund owns stock in. Some mutual funds also may require a high initial investment.

A mutual fund's performance history—its track record—can be obtained directly from the company or researched online. Generally, you'd want to invest in a mutual fund that has shown solid returns on investments for many years, not just one year or one quarter. In addition to money-losing mutual funds, you would want to avoid those whose fortunes have been volatile, sharply up one year and sharply down the next.

Buying real estate usually requires getting a loan, known as a mortgage, from a bank or other financial institution. A loan officer will determine whether you are a good candidate.

Real Estate: Investing in Land and Property

Investing in real estate, such as land, houses, and commercial or residential buildings, is difficult for teens because of the size of the initial investment that is usually required and the difficulty in obtaining a housing loan from a bank. It means buying a building or property today for a lot of cash and hoping that you can sell it later for more money than you paid for it. Real estate investments are something you'd have to do in conjunction with your parents or they would do on your behalf.

For many Americans, their biggest single investment is their home. Most people borrow money and get a loan—called

When the value of currency—such as the dollar—is weak, investors often buy up precious metals, like gold and silver. They are seen as having stable and enduring value in bad economic times.

a mortgage—to buy their house. As they pay off the loan, they earn equity. Equity is the value of their assets, or money, minus their debt, or what they still owe on the mortgage.

A lot of people buy property by getting a loan, which is extremely difficult for teens to do. However, if you are interested in investing in real state, you can consider a real estate investment trust, or REIT. REITs work like mutual funds, but they invest in many different properties instead of buying stock in many different companies.

The Commodities Market

Commodities are products, such as corn, soybeans, gold, silver, or oil. At commodity exchanges, instead of buying and selling stocks, which are ownership shares of companies, traders buy and sell contracts. The contracts are legal agreements to buy or sell commodities, such as wheat, at a future date. The hope is that when that day comes, you'll be able to sell your wheat for more than you agreed to pay for it today.

It's a bit complicated and difficult for teens to invest in commodities. If you are interested, though, take a look at the Web sites for the Chicago Mercantile Exchange or the Chicago Board of Trade to learn more about how commodities trading and futures contracts work and how people can get started investing in the markets.

CHAPTER FIVE

MUTUAL FUNDS: POOLING MONEY TO BUY STOCKS AND BONDS

While you are learning which individual companies you want to buy stock in, you can also consider buying into a mutual fund. Most states require that parents set up mutual fund accounts as a custodian if children are younger than the minimum age, which ranges from eighteen to twenty-two depending on the state.

MUTUAL FUNDS VS. THE STOCK MARKET

The average mutual fund earns about 2 percent less per year than the stock market performs in general, according to the Motley Fool Web site. Mutual funds also earn less than the market because of the fees shareholders can be charged. As with stocks, there are thousands of mutual funds you can invest in, and you could spend a lifetime researching which are the best ones. Remember, however, that there's no 100 percent accurate way to pick a mutual fund that will be a winner because no one knows what the future holds.

Shareholders in a mutual fund contribute to a pool of money. The mutual fund company uses this cash to buy stocks and bonds in other companies. The contributing members of the mutual fund then share in its financial successes and failures. If the fund performs poorly, all the shareholders lose money. If it performs well, all the shareholders receive a portion of the earnings.

A mutual fund's past performance is no guarantee of future performance. For example, just because the mutual fund boasted a 25 percent growth last year doesn't mean it won't struggle and lose money this year. As with any high-risk investment, you have the potential to earn a higher return than with a low-risk investment, such as a savings account, but you also run the risk of losing more money than you would in a lower-risk venture.

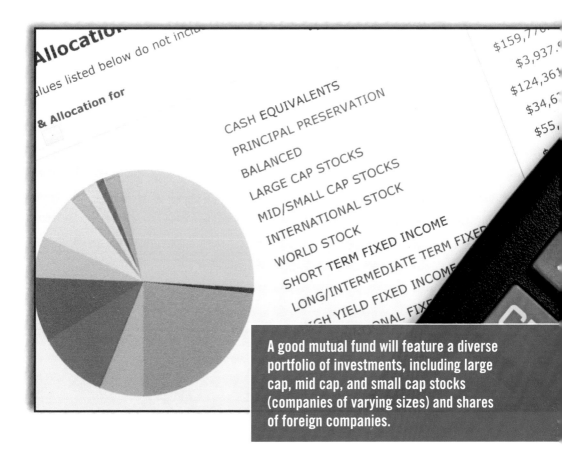

A good mutual fund will feature a diverse portfolio of investments, including large cap, mid cap, and small cap stocks (companies of varying sizes) and shares of foreign companies.

Diversifying Your Portfolio

Mutual funds allow investors to diversify, or spread out, their investments in a way they can't easily do by buying individual stocks. It's important to not carry all of your eggs in one basket because if something happens to that single basket, you'll lose your entire nest egg. Because mutual funds invest in so many diverse companies, if one single company does poorly, it may not hurt the mutual fund's overall performance.

Most funds require a minimum investment of $1,000 or more. Some newer mutual funds now cater to teens and invest

Publicly traded companies must make their annual reports and other information regarding their financial health and performance available to actual and potential investors. Researching and studying these reports can give you valuable insight into a company's current and future health.

in companies that young people know and like and whose products or services they use regularly.

The Wide World of Mutual Funds

Mutual funds come in many different forms, and there are thousands of individual ones from which to choose. Large cap funds invest in the 250 largest companies in the country. Mid cap funds invest in the next 750 largest companies. Small cap funds invest in smaller companies. Some funds are more aggressive, or risky, than others. But remember, with higher risk comes the potential for higher returns—or greater losses.

In a growth fund, the fund's manager invests in companies that are rapidly growing. In a value fund, the manager invests in companies he or she believes are strong but whose stock may be underpriced and poised to rise. A blend fund uses a combination of these two strategies. There are also funds that invest in international companies, and socially responsible funds, which don't invest in companies whose policies or practices harm the environment or people.

Mutual funds sometimes have "loads," or fees they charge an investor just to sign on. Look for a no-load mutual fund, although even these will have some fees to pay for the operation of the mutual fund. When buying into a mutual fund, you should also look at its expenses ratio. This is the proportion of assets that go toward paying for the administration of the fund. Funds that have lower administrative expenses are preferable, since less of the fund's profit is going to these costs and more is flowing back to the investors.

CHAPTER SIX

ALL ABOUT STOCKS

"**S**tocks are the best investments for anyone with a long-time horizon to save," says Selena Maranjian, of the financial Web site the Motley Fool. That's because over time, stocks tend to have a better rate of return than other types of investments. From 1900 to 2009, the stock market—as measured by the Dow Jones Industrial Average—has averaged a more than 9 percent yearly return on investment. For the last twenty-five years, the average annual rate of return has been almost 12 percent. In 2009, it was 22 percent for the year. From the stock market low of 2009 (following the crash of 2008) through 2010, the annual rate of return was a whopping 68 percent. Overall, stocks grow faster than Treasury bills and long-term government bonds.

Stocks tend not to be good short-term investments, however. While over time they have historically outperformed every other investment, in the short term, stocks can be a roller coaster ride that plummets as well as soars. In just one week in October 2008, for example, the stock market lost 18 percent of its value. That means people lost, not gained, money, and could have lost part of their principal investment.

Stock Prices

Companies raise money by selling stock, or ownership shares. Stocks range in price from less than $1 to thousands of dollars per share. The stock price is based on lots of different factors, including how the company is doing and whether people want to buy the stock.

In the world's biggest stock exchange, the New York Stock Exchange, traders buy and sell company shares in a giant auction. The price of stocks constantly changes, depending on how many people want to buy a specific stock compared to how many people want to sell it. This is the basic economic rule of supply and demand. If the supply is greater than the demand, the price falls. If the demand is greater than the supply, then there's not enough stock to go around and the price goes up. Once you have bought your stock, you want the price to go up. That means your share will be worth more than you paid for it, and if you sold it at that point, you'd make a profit. The

Traders on the floor of the New York Stock Exchange execute buy and sell orders that cause stock prices to rise and fall with the resulting fluctuations in supply and demand.

basic strategy for stock investment is to buy at a low price and sell at a high price—"buy low, sell high."

The Payoff: Dividends

When a company is profitable, the people who run the company may decide to share some of the profits with stockholders by issuing dividends. A dividend is a share of the company's profits that the company sends to its shareholders. Some companies allow you to use dividends to purchase additional shares of stock. This is called a dividend reinvestment program, or DRIP.

Stock Splits

When a company's stock reaches a certain price, the company's board of directors can also decide to split the stock. This can mean that instead of owning a single share worth $50, you could own two shares of stock each worth $25 if the stock splits. That keeps the stock affordable for more investors, encouraging more stock purchases and increasing share prices further.

How to Choose and Purchase a Stock

Some financial investors will tell you to invest in products or companies you know, use, or like. That's because buying a stock means becoming a part-owner in a company. If you are going to be a part-owner, make sure you like the company and would purchase its products. Chances are that if you like the company's product, many other people do, too. This kind of consumer satisfaction usually means the company is on a solid footing, does good work, and is creating innovative and desirable goods or services. This would seem to indicate it has a strong future and is a good investment.

There is no guaranteed, surefire way to tell if a stock will make money or lose money because no one knows what will happen in the future. There are thousands of ways to pick a company to invest in, but generally, you should look at the

Warner Wenning *(right)*, the chief executive officer of the chemical and pharmaceutical company Bayer, presents the company's annual report during a press conference.

company and judge how successful you think it will be. You can review a company's annual report, which is an update on how the company performed in the last year. You can talk to other investors, parents, teachers, and friends to see what they think.

If you're under eighteen, you may need some help—and good advice—from a parent or another adult to purchase stock. Parents can act as custodians for their children's stock under the Uniform Transfers to Minors Act. Here are some ways to buy stock:

- Go through a broker. This is a licensed professional who sells stocks. This can be expensive because most brokers charge a set fee whether you buy one share or one hundred. A lot of brokers may not want to sell you just a single share. If your parents or another responsible adult buys stock through a broker, you can ask them to tack on a share or two to one of their orders. A parent can also open a joint broker-age account that he or she can control until the child turns eighteen.
- Join or start an investment club. Some schools have programs through which kids can invest a small amount of money monthly. If your school doesn't have one, you can buy a youth membership with the National Association of Investors Corporation (NAIC), a nonprofit organization dedicated to teaching people how to invest. The NAIC has a youth investment club. For more information, check out its Web site.
- Some companies will let you buy stock directly from them, either with an initial purchase or through a dividend reinvestment program. Some companies may require an initial investment of $250 or more or require you to already own at least one share of stock.

47

CHAPTER SEVEN

STRATEGIES FOR SMART SAVING AND INVESTING

Successful saving and investing requires a lot of research, careful thought, and discipline. But the truth is it also requires a fair bit of luck. Even the wisest and most experienced investors will occasionally suffer losses, and some of the smartest people can spend or manage their money foolishly from time to time. But setbacks can be minimized by following some simple strategies for prudent investing and saving and avoiding common pitfalls.

One of the most important pieces of investing advice you will ever receive is do not fall for get-rich-quick schemes. There really is no such thing as a fast buck. Anything that sounds too good to be true probably is. Don't invest your money in anything you don't fully understand. And don't ever trust your money to anyone who is not representing a legitimate business that can be fully researched and evaluated.

Checking Accounts

A checking account is like a savings account. It, too, is a safe place to keep your money at the bank. Most checking accounts

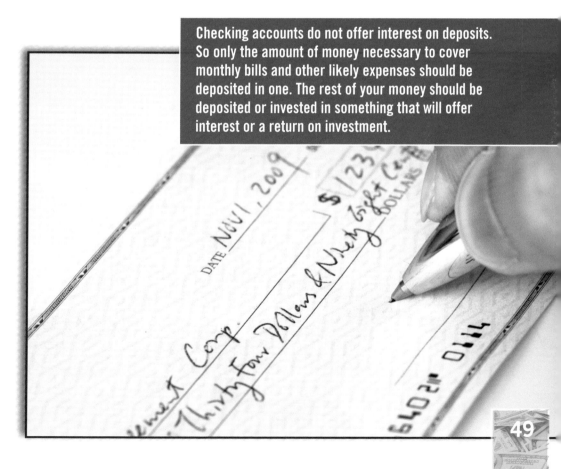

Checking accounts do not offer interest on deposits. So only the amount of money necessary to cover monthly bills and other likely expenses should be deposited in one. The rest of your money should be deposited or invested in something that will offer interest or a return on investment.

are not great places for saving money, however, because most banks don't offer interest on them. Many banks may actually charge you a fee to have a checking account. That's because checking accounts are about spending, not saving, money.

After you write a check or deposit money into your account, you add or subtract the amount from your balance. The balance is the amount of money you had in the account prior to writing a check or making a deposit. Balancing your account is very important because if you have insufficient funds in your account but continue to write checks, you will get into trouble. When you write a check for more money than you have, the bank will not honor it. A bad check is called a bounced check because the bank will not pay for it and it bounces back to you. The person or business to which you wrote the check will charge you an additional fee for writing the bad check. The bank will also punish you by charging a fee.

Writing bad checks can hurt your credit record, which is what companies and banks look at before deciding if you can have a credit card, car loan, or house loan. You may not need good credit today, but you will in the future. If you intentionally write bad checks, you can also face criminal charges.

The Dangers of Credit Cards: Debt

Borrowing money, while sometimes necessary, also has some dangers. Compound interest works both ways. You can earn it when saving money, but when borrowing money, you have to pay that interest back. So if you take a loan out from a bank for $1,000, with a 7 percent interest rate, compounded annually, you will owe $70 in interest at year's end, even before you begin paying back the initial $1,000 borrowed.

Credit cards are actually a form of borrowing. Whenever you charge a purchase to a credit card, you are essentially borrowing money from the credit card company, usually at a very high interest rate that is compounded monthly. Some teens have credit cards they obtained themselves or through their parents' accounts. Credit cards are dangerous because it's easy to adopt a "spend today, pay tomorrow" attitude. You should never use a credit card for anything for which you can't afford to pay cash today. They should be used as a convenience—so you don't have to make a withdrawal or carry cash when shopping—not as a means of buying something expensive you couldn't otherwise pay for.

Credit cards can charge hefty interest fees, which means you are paying far more than just the sticker price of the things you buy. People mistakenly believe that they can effectively manage their credit card debt by making just the small, minimum payment every month. If you do this, you are actually digging yourself into a hole of debt you may never climb out of. If you carry a $3,000 balance on a credit card with a 19.8 percent interest rate and pay the required minimum balance of 3 percent each month, or $15 (whichever is higher), it would take you thirty-nine years to pay off the loan. Interest would keep accruing on the unpaid portion of the balance, which would no doubt be increasing as you purchase more goods.

Avoiding Hidden Fees and Charges

Be on the lookout for hidden fees and charges. Ask the bank if your savings account has a charge for withdrawals or other account activity or if there are any penalties that kick in when your balance dips below a certain level. Ask your mutual fund manager how much the fund will charge you to set up an account and what the fees or penalties are when you cash out. Watch out for credit card companies that will charge you to borrow money. If any bank, mutual fund, or credit card company seems to impose a lot of charges and penalties for normal account activity, don't do business with it. Shop around for low-fee service providers instead. Research is the key. Carefully read all terms and conditions associated with a bank account, credit card, investment fund, or other financial account.

A Family Affair

What if your parents don't know much about investing? You have to teach them. Working together and coming to a consensus on how to invest family money can be a great learning opportunity for all involved. Together you can research investment opportunities, debate their merits, and weigh the risks versus the rewards. Two or more heads are better than one. The wisdom of the group tends to result in better investment performance than that achieved by a lone investor doing all the research, analysis, deliberation, and decision-making himself or herself.

Investing and Saving with Twenty-First Century Skills and Tools

Learning about potential investments and financial services, understanding the investment and saving process, and managing one's investments and financial accounts have never been easier than they are now. Twenty-first century technology allows ordinary individual investors the opportunity to research, scrutinize, and discuss potential investments from their home computers, laptops, or smartphones. Even the actual transactions and account management can be done online.

There are numerous reputable Web sites that offer users expert investment and money management advice, as well as helpful warnings about common dangers. For example, the Investing Online Resource Center is sponsored by the North American Securities Administrators Association. Its main mission is the education and protection of ordinary, individual investors. Among other things, the Investing Online Resource Center shows users what it's like to trade online, how investment accounts work, and how investors can protect themselves online. It teaches users things every investor should know, such as how to open an online account and how to choose an online brokerage firm. It also gives users tips about how to avoid identity theft, online scams, and investment fraud.

A similar online service is provided by the Securities and Exchange Commission. This government agency provides a Beginner's Guide to Investing that contains numerous Web links to its online publications. Archived articles concern roadmaps to savings and investment, questions to ask about your investments, what to do if you get into trouble with your investments, how to straighten out your finances, tools for comparing mutual funds, advice from security industry regulators, how to choose brokers, how to read financial statements, and how to obtain information about companies.

Online investing has become enormously popular in recent years, allowing individuals to take control of their own investing decisions and develop their own strategies. These sites include E*Trade, TD Ameritrade, ShareBuilder, Scottrade, and the online sites of established brokerages like Fidelity, Charles Schwab, and Vanguard. They offer free independent research, customer support, trading and investing education, professional investment guidance, online advisers, streaming quotes and charts, retirement and banking services, and the ability to trade in stocks, bonds, mutual funds, commodities, and futures.

All you have to do is open an account with one of these online brokers, and you are ready to begin researching and investing. Make sure you check the Web site's Terms of Use page to see if there are any age restrictions for use of the services. Always use these online investing tools with the help and consultation of a parent or other responsible adult. Online investing has made the process easy—almost too easy. It is possible to spend and lose an awful lot of money very quickly with these sites and without an actual broker advising and cautioning you every step of the way.

A SIMPLE STRATEGY FOR SAVING AND INVESTING SUCCESS

Here are a few quick saving and investment tips:

- Comparison shop: Just as you should spend your money carefully and price check anything you want to buy in several different places, you should also comparison shop to find the best bank, best mutual fund, and best investment to put your money in.
- Diversity: Don't carry your entire nest egg in one basket. It's good to have investments in several places. That helps diversify the risk you are carrying and minimize potential losses.
- Don't get overwhelmed: This is a lot of information to digest. If you feel overwhelmed, don't give up and do nothing. Start at the beginning. Make a budget. Start to save. Put your money in the bank, and keep studying investments until you feel comfortable enough to begin investing. Start small. Save a little every month. Then buy a stock or two. Eventually invest in a mutual fund.
- Patience is a virtue: You have the power to become financially secure, even wealthy. But it will not happen overnight. You have the most valuable tool of all: time. Be patient, and remember that the earlier you start saving and investing, the longer your money will have to grow.

Take advantage of other digital tools by keeping track of your savings and investments with the help of a computer spreadsheet program (like Excel, Numbers, Calc, or Gnumeric). You can even use programs that create graphic organizers like bar graphs and pie charts to get a better visual sense of how your money is being spent or growing and how the investments—individually and collectively—are performing over time. Recording all your financial activity in spreadsheets and accompanying graphic organizers will help you be more aware of how much money is being spent and saved, where it is being spent, what fees and charges have been paid, if you are staying within budget, and which investments are performing well or poorly.

All of this information can then be used to guide your saving and investing strategy and decisions going forward. It's a brave new digital world of saving and investing! Go out and explore it carefully, wisely, and with adult guidance, advice, and oversight.

bond A loan to companies or governments. Buyers of bonds receive interest on their investment.

broker An individual who is paid a fee or commission for executing buy or sell orders for a customer. A broker can manage client accounts, make trade recommendations, and place trades.

certificate of deposit (CD) A bank investment for a set period of time at a set interest rate.

commodities exchange A place where various goods and products are traded.

commodity A good that is sold before being processed, such as wheat, tobacco, or cotton.

compound interest New interest that is earned or charged on the principal and the old interest.

debt Something that is owed or that one is bound to pay to or perform for another person.

demand A desire for a particular good or product.

dividend A small share of profits that a company pays to stockholders.

dividend reinvestment program (DRIP) A program that allows investors to use their dividends to buy additional stock.

futures contract An agreement to buy or sell a certain commodity, at a certain time in the future, to be delivered to a certain place.

inflation An increase in the amount of money needed to buy things.

interest A sum paid or charged for the use of money or for borrowing money; often expressed as a percentage of money borrowed and to be paid back within a given time.

investor A person who spends money on a company or enterprise and expects to make a profit in return.

principal Seed money; the amount of the original investment before interest.

public company A company that sells shares of its ownership to the public.

risk How safe an investor's principal is. Generally, low-risk investments earn low interest, and high-risk investments earn high interest. The potential for a big gain, however, also means the potential for a big loss.

securities Certificates of stocks that prove a person's partial ownership of a company.

shares Units of ownership in a company; a share of stock.

split The breaking up or dividing of stocks in order to lower per share prices.

stock A portion or share of ownership in a company that is traded publicly.

stock market Where stocks are bought and sold, or traded.

supply The total amount of a specific good that is available to consumers.

trading The buying and selling of stocks.

volatility A measurement of the change in price or value of a given stock, bond, mutual fund, or other investment over a specific period of time.

American Association of Individual Investors (AAII)
625 North Michigan Avenue
Chicago, IL 60611
(800) 428-2244
Web site: http://www.aaii.com
The AAII is a nonprofit organization that provides education for
individual investors so that they can effectively manage their own
stock portfolios.

Department of Finance Canada
140 O'Connor Street
19th Floor, East Tower
Ottawa, ON K1A 0G5
Canada
(613) 992-1573
Web site: http://www.fin.gc.ca
The Department of Finance Canada plans and prepares the budget
for the Canadian government. It also establishes rules and regu-
lations for Canadian banks and finance institutions.

National Endowment for Financial Education
5299 DTC Boulevard, Suite 1300
Greenwood Village, CO 80111
(303) 741-6333
Web site: http://www.nefe.org
This organization is a private, nonprofit, national foundation devoted
to educating Americans about finance and improving their financial well-being. The organization includes an educational
program for high school students.

New York Stock Exchange (NYSE)
11 Wall Street
New York, NY 10005

(212) 656-3000

Web site: http://www.nyse.com

The NYSE is the world's largest exchange group and offers the most diverse array of financial products and services.

Toronto Stock Exchange

First Canadian Place

77 Adelaide Street West

Toronto, ON M5X 1A4

Canada

(888) 873-8392

Web site: http://www.tmx.com

The Toronto Stock Exchange was established in 1852 and continues to help companies become listed in a world market. It also helps investors enter the world market.

U.S. Securities and Exchange Commission (SEC)

100 F Street NE

Washington, DC 20549

(202) 942-8088

Web site: http://www.sec.gov

The SEC oversees the activities of stock exchanges and stockbrokers. It aims to protect investors and keep the trading of stocks as fair and orderly as possible.

Web Sites

Due to the changing nature of Internet links, Rosen Publishing has developed an online list of Web sites related to the subject of this book. This site is updated regularly. Please use this link to access the list:

http://www.rosenlinks.com/dol/sai

FOR FURTHER READING

Clifford, Tim. *Our Economy in Action*. Vero Beach, FL: Rourke Publishing, 2009.

Craats, Rennay. *Economy: USA Past Present Future*. New York, NY: Weigl Publishers, 2009.

Deatherage, Judi. *Who Wants to Be a Millionaire?* Lexington, KY: The Clark Group, 2007.

Fradin, Dennis Brindell, and Judith Bloom Fradin. *Investing*. Tarrytown, NY: Marshall Cavendish, 2010.

Furgang, Kathy. *How the Stock Market Works* (Real World Economics). New York, NY: Rosen Publishing, 2011.

Hall, Alvin. *Show Me the Money: How to Make Cents of Economics*. New York, NY: DK, 2008.

Karlitz, Gail, and Debbie Honig. *Growing Money: A Complete Investing Guide for Kids*. New York, NY: Price Stern Sloan, 2010.

Krantz, Matt. *Investing Online for Dummies*. Hoboken, NJ: Wiley Publishing, 2008.

La Bella, Laura. *How Commodities Trading Works* (Real World Economics). New York, NY: Rosen Publishing, 2011.

Meyer, Susan. *How Buying and Selling Futures Works* (Real World Economics). New York, NY: Rosen Publishing, 2011.

Minden, Celia. *Investing: Making Your Money Work for You*. Ann Arbor, MI: Cherry Lake Publishing, 2007.

Mladjenovic, Paul. *Stock Investing for Dummies*. Hoboken, NJ: Wiley Publishing, 2009.

Morrison, Jessica. *Investing*. New York, NY: Weigl Publishers, 2009.

Orr, Tamra. *A Kid's Guide to Stock Market Investing*. Hockessin, DE: Mitchell Lane Publishers, 2008.

Tyson, Eric. *Investing for Dummies*. 5th ed. Hoboken, NJ: Wiley Publishing, 2008.

INDEX

A

automated teller machines (ATMs), 24

B

bankruptcy, 28
Barnum, P. T., 15
blend funds, 41
bonds, 17, 24, 28, 32–33, 38, 54
bounced checks, 50
brokers, 47, 54
budgets, 7, 8, 56

C

certificates of deposit, 26
Charles Schwab, 54
checking accounts, 28, 49–50
Chicago Board of Trade, 36
Chicago Mercantile Exchange, 36
collectibles, 28, 33
commodities, 28, 36, 54
compound interest, 9, 16, 18–19,
    50–51
credit cards, 50–51, 52
credit records, 50
credit unions, 28

D

debt, 36, 50, 51
deposit insurance, 28, 30
dividend reinvestment program (DRIP),
    45, 47
dividends, 44–45, 47
Dow Jones Industrial Average, 42

E

eBay, 11
equity, 36

E*trade, 54
expense ratios, 41

F

Federal Deposit Insurance Corporation
    (FDIC), 28
fees and charges, hidden, 52
Fidelity, 54
Franklin, Benjamin, 18
futures, 36, 54

G

get-rich-quick schemes, 8, 49
growth funds, 41

I

impulse purchases, 9
inflation, 19, 21, 30
Investing Online Resource Center, 53
investment clubs, 47

J

joint brokerage accounts, 47

L

large cap funds, 41
Leech, Irene, 8
loans, 27, 28, 30, 32, 35–36, 50, 51

M

Maranjian, Selena, 6, 42
mid cap funds, 41
money management basics, 7–14
money market funds, 24–25, 26
mortgages, 35–36
Motley Fool, 6, 38, 42

About the Authors

David W. Berg is a writer who lives in New York City.

Meg Green is a writer and journalist who has written on numerous financial topics, including *Everything You Need to Know About Credit Cards and Fiscal Responsibility*.

Photo Credits

Cover, pp. 7, 15, 22, 27, 37, 42, 48 © www.istockphoto.com/ monkeypics; interior graphics © www.istockphoto.com/mecaleha; background of page numbers istockphoto/Thinkstock; p. 5 Picturenet/ Blend Images/Getty Images; p. 9 Savingforcollege.com; p. 11 Digital Vision/Thinkstock; p. 13 Howard Grey/Stone/Getty Images; pp. 17, 44 Bloomberg/Bloomberg via Getty Images; pp. 20, 40 David Young-Wolff/Photo Edit; pp. 23, 31, 39, 49 Shutterstock; p. 25 © Bill Aron/Photo Edit; p. 29 Bob Daemmrich/The Image Works; p. 34 Larry Dale Gordon/Stone/Getty Images; p. 35 Photos.com/ Jupiterimages/Thinkstock; p. 46 © AP Images.

Designer: Nicole Russo; Photo Researcher: Marty Levick

12/28/11